LOVERS
IN ART

LOVERS
IN ART

IAIN ZACZEK

Picture selection by
Julia Brown

STUDIO EDITIONS
LONDON

Frontispiece: William Dyce (1806—64),
Paola and Francesca *(detail).*

This edition published 1994 by
Studio Editions Ltd
Princess House, 50 Eastcastle Street
London, W1N 7AP, England

Design by Michael R Carter
Printed and bound in the Slovak Republic

ISBN 1 85891 173 7

INTRODUCTION

The depiction of love plays a significant role in the history of Western art. The emotion is universal, after all, and no culture can ignore it. Even so, European artists have been constrained by certain taboos and this has given rise to a curiously divided tradition.

The serious aspects of love were governed by Christian ethics and, in particular, by the concept of original sin, which was closely allied to Adam and Eve's failure to resist sexual temptation. As a result, from medieval times they were normally portrayed as transgressors rather than lovers, and their offence spawned a broad repertoire of negative love imagery. For example, lustful couples featured in scenes of the Damnation in many altarpieces, and were the focus of a type of morality painting that flourished long after the Middle Ages.

Marital love was, of course, exempt from these strictures. Marriage was one of the sacraments and it was perfectly possible to depict couples in the matrimonial bed without fear of censure. However, there was precious little joy or affection in

Roman de la Rose, c. 1500, Flemish. Bel Acueil (Fair
Welcome) shows Lover the rose.

many of these pictures. *The Arnolfini Wedding* (*see* Plate 3) has the solemnity of a religious icon, while the wedding night of Sarah and Tobias (*see* Plate 6) displays none of the exuberance that one would expect. Even in an entirely secular betrothal painting, the emphasis tended to be on the importance of the dynastic alliance rather than on the happiness of the event.

Where sensual lovers were depicted, there was often a suggestion that their enjoyment would be short-lived. This was easy to convey in a series of pictures — as in Hogarth's *Rake's Progress*, which illustrates the tale of a self-indulgent youth getting his come-uppance — but much less straight-forward in a single image. In many instances, therefore, embracing couples were used as a visual shorthand to signify moral laxity. As a result artists faced the problem of portraying physical love. They did not have the freedom that was available in other cultures to depict its erotic nature. Indian miniaturists, for example, could depict the sexual act in graphic detail, unencum-bered by any moral constraints. An erotic tradition did exist in the West, but it was a covert practice, unacceptable as part of the artistic mainstream.

Instead, love was usually portrayed through an elaborate system of symbols and conventions. Many of these sprang out of the courtly love phenomenon, which permeated all the art forms of medieval Europe, ranging from the love songs of the troubadours to rambling verse epics, such as the *Roman de la Rose*. The latter proved an enormously popular subject with artists and many

Mars and Venus, *vitrine miniature from the Spanish room at Kingston Lacy, Dorset. Cupid prepares to fire his arrow, as the god of war falls victim to the charms of Venus.*

of its themes outlived the vogue for the book itself. The action of the *Roman de la Rose* took place within a garden and this rapidly became a standard setting for the representation of idealized love. Painters as diverse as Giorgione, Rubens and Watteau all produced romantic outdoor idylls.

Another amorous metaphor which had gained wide currency during the Middle Ages was the 'citadel of love'. Here, knights laid siege to a castle defended by women. Distant echoes of this picturesque allegory about the pitfalls of courtship can be detected in paintings from succeeding centuries, as in the way that Fragonard's young lover (see Plate 11) and Madox Brown's Romeo (see Plate 14) have to surmount physical barriers in order to claim their prize.

An equally popular comparison could be made with love and music. Poetic parallels were drawn between the act of seduction and a music lesson, while pictures with titles like *The Duet*, *The Concert* or *Harmony* alluded to a successful outcome. Once again, the subject had a long pedigree. Medieval astrologers had classified musicians under the planetary influence of Venus, and illustrations of the relevant zodiacal sign (Taurus) invariably showed scenes of couples taking their pleasure in music, dancing and love-making.

With the rediscovery of Classical learning during the Renaissance, Venus came to play an increasing role in the visual arts. The ancient myths were used as allegories of the latest philosophical trends, and one of the most familiar themes was 'Venus subduing Mars'. This represented the notion that 'love conquers strife' and usually showed the triumphant goddess lulling her quarrelsome partner to sleep. Sometimes, she was attended by Cupid or by small *putti*, who amused themselves by playing with the god of war's weapons and armour.

The use of these emblems of love remained commonplace until the nineteenth century

although, increasingly, attempts were made to incorporate them naturalistically into the scene. Accordingly, *putti* were often included as background paintings, as statuary or as architectural details (*see* Plates 8 & 11).

Even so, most portrayals of love still possessed a strong escapist element. Amorous couples were often shown wearing costumes or masks, and played out their flirtatious games in fairyland settings. This trend persisted well into the Victorian era, when many artists chose to depict romance in the guise of history (*see* Plate 16) or as a scene from literature. Shakespeare, Dante and Keats were their favourite sources.

Some Victorian painters, however, preferred to tackle the theme of love in a modern context. The results were often sentimental, but there were also brave attempts to confront serious issues, such as adultery, prostitution and broken marriages. These efforts were redoubled by the Impressionists, who made a point of portraying scenes from modern life, and, by the end of the century, artists were finally producing images of genuine, unadorned passion.

Opposite: Engraving after Jean-Frederic Schall (1752–1825), The Lover Surprised. *This playful flirtation recalls the old saying that 'love is blind'.*

— THE —
PLATES

PLATE 1

Sienese School (14th century)
The Dangers of Love

DETAIL

This bathing scene is one of a series of frescoes in the Palazzo del Popolo in San Gimignano. The scheme is situated in the private chamber of the *podestà* (a high-ranking official) and was only discovered during restoration work in 1921. The room itself dates from the early fourteenth century and the paintings were probably added soon afterwards. They have been attributed to various different artists, but the most likely candidate is Memmo di Filippuccio.

Most of the frescoes are of a decidedly erotic nature. Other scenes show Aristotle with a courtesan, and a youth being lured into a tent and robbed by a group of women, and the indications are that the paintings were intended as a moral warning against the dangers of illicit love. The present image is the central episode in a three-part story. In the first scene a young nobleman is ushered into a house, while the final picture shows him climbing into bed with a naked woman, who is already asleep. Her lack of interest suggests that she may be a prostitute.

PLATE 2

Arras Tapestry (*c.* 1400–10)
The Offering of the Heart

The scene depicted here is an episode from the *Roman de la Rose*, the enormously popular French poem which epitomized the chivalrous code of courtly love. The *Roman* was begun in *c.* 1237 by Guillaume de Lorris and was completed some 40 years later by Jean de Meun, but its influence extended well into the fifteenth century. It tells the story of a lover entering a utopian garden, where he pays court to his heart's desire, symbolized by a beautiful rosebud. After passing an elaborate series of tests, he is allowed to pluck the bloom (the lady). Ultimately, the *Roman* was about ideas rather than people. Thus, for example, *Bel Acueil* (Fair Welcome) was portrayed as either a woman or a man, depending on the context of the story.

This was an appropriate subject for tapestries, which served a practical purpose by reducing draughts, but were also important status symbols. Courtly romances were a popular theme because they affirmed the aristocratic way of life. It is significant that the suitor was welcomed into the Garden of Love by *Oiseuse* (Leisure), while a figure like Poverty was excluded as an undesirable.

PLATE 3

Jan van Eyck (*d.* 1441)
The Arnolfini Wedding

This famous portrait depicts Giovanni Arnolfini, a prosperous financier from Lucca, together with his French-born wife, Jeanne Cenami. The picture is not only a record of their wedding, but also a celebration of the sacrament of marriage. The man's hand is raised to signify his vow, and his expression reflects the solemnity of the undertaking. Van Eyck has underlined this by adding a wealth of symbolic detail. The dog is a common token of marital fidelity and, on the top of the chair, there is a tiny statuette of St Margaret, the patron saint of childbirth. The fruit on the window ledge is a reminder of mankind's state of innocence before the Fall. The single candle burning in the chandelier, which serves no practical purpose as the scene takes place in broad daylight, is a marriage candle. This was sometimes carried at the head of a bridal procession or was formally presented by the groom to his new wife.

PLATE 4

Fra Filippo Lippi (*c.* 1406—69)
A Man and Woman at a Casement

This is one of the earliest surviving double portraits from the Italian Renaissance and it seems probable that it was commissioned to mark either a wedding or a betrothal. Many attempts have been made to identify the couple, but the only firm evidence suggests that the man was a member of the Scolari family. Their coat of arms can be seen on the cloth beneath his hands. Some embroidered letters can be seen at the edge of the woman's sleeve — probably part of her family motto — but her name remains a mystery.

The painting used to be attributed to Masaccio, but is now normally ascribed to Lippi. The latter's own lifestyle would merit inclusion in any book about lovers. He was an unwanted child and was raised as an unwilling friar by the Carmelites. However, he was released from his vows after embarking on a scandalous affair with a nun, Lucrezia Buti. Apparently, he had conducted the romance while using the girl as his model for a picture of the Virgin Mary.

PLATE 5
Hugo van der Goes (*d.* 1482)
The Fall

Adam and Eve have probably inspired more paintings than any other couple, although the emphasis has rarely been on their status as lovers. For the artists of Hugo's time, the theme was popular for two main reasons. It was, of course, a fundamental part of the Biblical story and it also provided painters with one of their few opportunities of depicting the nude. Hugo's version forms part of a diptych, together with a Lamentation over Christ. This pairing is entirely logical, as Adam and Eve's disobedience was regarded as the original sin, which had to be redeemed by Christ's crucifixion. The human figures owe something to Van Eyck, but the anthropomorphic serpent is a wonderful invention, its female features reflecting the misogynistic attitudes of contemporary theologians. The iris, like the lily, was a symbol of purity in Netherlandish art and its strategic positioning here acts as a reminder of the state of innocence which Eve is about to lose.

PLATE 6

German School (16th century)
Tobias and Sarah

A hidden drama lurks behind this seemingly placid scene. The subject comes from the Book of Tobit in the Apocrypha, which is a blend of two ancient folk myths (the Grateful Dead and the Dangerous Bride). It is the second of these legends which is relevant here. Sarah had been married seven times, but each of her husbands had been killed on their wedding night by the demon Asmodeus. However, with the assistance of an angel, Tobias overcame this adversary and spent the night safely with his new wife.

It is interesting to compare this stained glass window with *The Arnolfini Wedding* (*see* Plate 3) to see how many marital symbols are repeated. The dog and the candle appear in both scenes, and even the discarded pattens have a concealed meaning (their prominent position in the Van Eyck painting confirms that their purpose is symbolic). The reference here is to the Biblical quotation in the Book of Exodus, "Put off thy shoes from off thy feet, for the place whereon thou standest is holy ground".

PLATE 7

Rembrandt van Rijn (1606—69)
The Jewish Bride

DETAIL

The title of this celebrated double portrait is a nineteenth-century invention. Almost certainly, Rembrandt modelled the composition on a genuine bridal pair, but their unusual gestures suggest that he was portraying his patrons in the guise of a Biblical couple. The protective attitude of the man is reminiscent of contemporary depictions of Jacob and Rachel, but most authorities believe that the artist's real theme was the story of Isaac and Rebecca from the Book of Genesis. While residing in the country of the Philistines, the former tried to pass Rebecca off as his sister rather than his wife, fearing that a jealous local might kill him in order to ravish her. However, this pretence was exposed when the Philistine king saw the lovers embracing. He rebuked Isaac for the deceit and guaranteed the couple's safety. The true identity of the sitters has never been discovered, although some critics have suggested that they might be the artist's son, Titus, and his bride, Magdalena van Loo, who were married in 1668.

PLATE 8

Johannes Vermeer (1632—75)
Lady standing at the Virginals

Artists in seventeenth-century Holland approached the subject of love elliptically, often using sophisticated allegories to convey their message. One of their favourite conceits involved the association of love with music. Accordingly, subjects like 'The Duet' or 'The Music Lesson' were invariably coded representations of lovers. Vermeer made extensive use of this metaphor, frequently adorning his painted domestic interiors with pictures that subtly reinforced his point.

The key to the meaning of this particular work lies in the large painting on the far wall. Here, we see a copy of a picture attributed to Cesar van Everdingen, which appears in several of Vermeer's canvases. It depicts Cupid, the god of love, holding up a single playing card. This, in turn, was based on an engraving from Otto van Veen's *Emblems of Love*. There, the image was accompanied by the motto, *Perfectus Amor Est Nisi ad Unum* (the perfect love is for one lover alone). For this reason, some critics have interpreted the present scene as either an engagement picture or a symbolic declaration of love.

PLATE 9
William Hogarth (1697–1764)
Before *and* After

Hogarth's work bridged the worlds of satire and art and here, in one of his earliest compositions, the air of parody is unmistakable. *Before* is strongly reminiscent of the *fêtes galantes* (courtship parties), which had been popularized by painters like Watteau and Mercier. In this elegant but artificial genre, trysting lovers were shown disporting themselves in idyllic parkland settings. Hogarth undermined the convention, however, by adding the second painting, in which the ungainly, post-coital disarray of the lovers destroyed any pretence of refinement. The artist produced another version of the theme, but translated the action to a fashionable interior.

Appropriately enough, *Before* and *After* were closely linked to scandal. They were commissioned by John Thomson, MP for Great Marlow and an administrator of the Charitable Corporation for the Relief of the Industrious Poor. In 1731, he fled to France after embezzling money from the latter and never collected his paintings.

PLATE 10
Arthur Devis (1711−87)
An Incident in the
Grounds of Ranelagh

The incident referred to in the title occurred when a lady and gentleman met at a masked ball. They enjoyed each other's company so much that, after the dance, they decided to unmask. On doing so, they were astonished to find that they were husband and wife. Judging by their expressions, the revelation was not entirely welcome. The figures in the painting were William Henry Ricketts and his wife Mary. Whether or not the anecdote was true, Ricketts appears to have been fond of Ranelagh. He had a second portrait painted there, wearing the same mask and costume.

The pleasure gardens at Ranelagh opened in 1742 and rapidly became one of London's most popular night spots. Here, we see the ornamental lake and the huge rotunda, where crowds gathered to eat, drink and listen to the music. It was an ideal setting for romance and Edward Gibbon called it "the most convenient place for courtships of every kind − the best market we have in England".

Wᵐ Henry Rickett.   Mary Rickett, Née Jervis.

PLATE 11

Jean-Honoré Fragonard (1732−1806)
The Surprise

This is one of a series of paintings known collectively as *The Progress of Love*. They were originally commissioned in 1771 by Louis XV's mistress, Madame du Barry, for her new pavilion at Louveciennes. Two years later, however, she rejected the scheme and the paintings were eventually installed in the house of Fragonard's cousin in Grasse.

The scene depicts a young man climbing up a ladder to meet his beloved on a terrace. In her right hand she holds a letter, which may be a message arranging this assignation. However, something has interrupted their tryst, as both figures look in alarm to the left. This situation is confirmed by the statue, which shows Venus disarming Cupid − a signal that love must be delayed. The key to this interruption may lie in the intended location of the painting, on the right-hand side of the door leading into Madame du Barry's garden. Thus, when any of her visitors passed through this door, it would have created the illusion that it was they who were disturbing the lovers' rendezvous.

PLATE 12

Thomas Rowlandson (1756–1827)
A Milk Sop

It would be a mistake to think that every artist treated love in either a serious or poetic manner. Satirists like Hogarth and Rowlandson used the theme to mirror the foibles of their age. Their respective approaches, however, were entirely different. Hogarth's tone was usually moralizing and censorious, whereas Rowlandson's sympathies were always with the lusty young lovers. Here, for example, the butt of his humour was not the young student who leans out of the window to sieze a kiss, but the crabby old don who looks on in disgust. The lad's good fortune is echoed by that of the dog on the left, which takes advantage of the situation by lapping up some cream from the milkmaid's pail. Rowlandson's allegiances may seem strange, given that he was 55 when he produced this design, but he always retained nostalgic memories of his own uproarious youth. Indeed, it was in this period that he produced his most flagrantly pornographic designs – many of them for the Prince Regent, the future George IV.

PLATE 13

François Gérard (1770–1837)
Cupid and Psyche

The story of these mismatched lovers was related in the *Golden Ass* by Apuleius. Reports of Psyche's beauty had stirred Venus to jealousy and she dispatched Cupid to punish the girl, by causing her to become infatuated with some hideous creature. Instead, Cupid himself fell victim to her charms and took her as his lover. However, he kept his divine nature a secret, only visiting Psyche by night and forbidding her to look at him. Eventually, though, her curiosity overcame her and she fetched a lamp to gaze at him while he slept. Angered at her disobedience, Cupid abandoned her.

Gérard's principal interest was in portraying the sculptural nude figures, but the subject presented him with obvious practical problems. He could scarcely set the action in a darkened room, and so transferred it into an improbable landscape. He also found it hard to convey the fact that Psyche could not see her lover and this explains her vacant expression and her muted reaction to Cupid's caresses. An incidental touch is that *psyche* is Greek for butterfly — hence the one fluttering above her head.

PLATE 14

Ford Madox Brown (1821−93)
Romeo and Juliet

This watercolour illustrates the reluctant parting of the lovers in Act III of Shakespeare's play. Juliet says, "Wilt thou begone, it is not yet near day?", while her partner points to the streaks of dawn that are lighting up the sky and begins to clamber down his rope-ladder. There are, of course, earlier versions of this subject, but the Victorians brought a fresh approach to Shakespearean themes. Instead of depicting them as theatrical performances, they tended to portray them as genuine, historical events.

A romantic story lies behind the picture. The model for Romeo was Charles Augustus Howell, the critic Ruskin's private secretary and an agent for several of the Pre-Raphaelites. He posed for the painting in the months before his own wedding in August 1867. Madox Brown's daughters were bridesmaids at the ceremony. The circumstances of the 'Juliet' were less happy. She was the artist's second wife, Emma, and, at the time the scene was painted, their marriage was under considerable strain.

PLATE 15

Jean-Léon Gérôme (1824–1904)
Pygmalion and Galatea

The legend of Pygmalion was familiar to nineteenth-century painters from Ovid's *Metamorphoses*. According to this, he was a Cypriot who, appalled by the lax morals of the women of his time, had decided to remain a bachelor. In his seclusion, he carved an ivory statue of his vision of the feminine ideal and prayed to Venus to send him a similar mate. She consented and, when he kissed the statue, it turned into a real woman.

Gérôme was a sculptor as well as a painter and the story therefore had a special significance for him. He painted several versions of it, using his studio as the setting. As a result, some of the items in the picture are recognizable as his own works. Gérôme also produced a sculpture on this theme, which was exhibited at the Paris Salon of 1892. This depicted the transformation scene and both the figures were tinted, although, as here, Galatea was only coloured above the waist.

PLATE 16
John Everett Millais (1829−96)
The Huguenot

The full title of this work is *A Huguenot, on St Bartholomew's Day, Refusing to Shield Himself from Danger by Wearing the Roman Catholic Badge*. The painting is based on an actual event — some 50,000 Huguenots (French Protestants) were massacred on St Bartholomew's Day in 1572 — but Millais' immediate source was Meyerbeer's opera, *Les Huguenots*. In this, the Catholic heroine fails to persuade her Protestant lover to betray his faith, by wearing the popish white cloth on his arm, and so decides to join him in his martyrdom. The artist underlined the tragedy of this tale by adding appropriate plants to the wall in the background. In the language of flowers, ivy stands for friendship in adversity, while the Canterbury bell can allude to constancy or faith.

The model for the female figure had just undergone a throat operation, which may account for the slightly clumsy positioning of the man's hands. Despite this, the painting attracted huge crowds when exhibited at the Royal Academy and marked the public acceptance of Millais, following the furore that had surrounded his association with the Pre-Raphaelite Brotherhood.

PLATE 17

Arthur Hughes (1830–1915)
The Long Engagement

This is Victorian painting at its most sentimental. A middle-aged couple are shown visiting their former meeting-place, where the man had once carved the woman's name, Amy, on a tree trunk. However, this is now overgrown with foliage, indicating that their youthful hopes have been disappointed. Something, perhaps a lack of money, has prevented them from marrying and the realization causes them both distress. When Hughes exhibited the painting in 1859, he presented it with a quotation from Chaucer's *Troilus and Criseyde* instead of a title:

> *For how myght ever sweetness hav be*
> * known*
> *To hym that never tastyd bitterness...*

Initially, however, he had intended to depict a scene in the Forest of Arden from Shakespeare's *As You Like It*, before deciding that a couple in modern dress would have more impact. Like Millais, Hughes created tender, romantic images, but did not feel entirely comfortable until he had placed them in a literary context.

PLATE 18

Edward Burne-Jones (1833–98)
Love Among the Ruins

DETAIL

A t first glance, this looks like another painting culled from a literary source. Indeed,
there is a poem by Browning with the same
title, but its relevance to the picture is open to
question. It tells the story of a shepherd meeting
his beloved on the barren site of a once-great city,
concluding that, in spite of all the wealth and glory
that this stronghold had possessed, 'love is best'.
Here, however, the moral seems reversed. The
lovers seem fearful and cling to each other
protectively, as if aware that their affections may
prove as fragile and ephemeral as the ruins
surrounding them. As was his custom, Burne-
Jones preferred to evoke a mood rather than a
specific theme. He was clearly pleased with the
result, as this painting was a copy of a gouache
that he had executed some 20 years earlier. He
decided to produce it when the original was
damaged in a photographer's studio.

PLATE 19

Auguste Rodin (1840–1917)
The Kiss

This is probably the most celebrated embrace in Western art but, even though the image is unforgettable, it emerged as an accidental offshoot of a separate project. In 1880, Rodin received an important state commission to design a bronze door for a new museum that was to be devoted to the decorative arts. His chosen theme was a 'Gate of Hell', which was to feature episodes from Dante's *Inferno*. One of these was the tragic love story of Paolo Malatesta and Francesca da Rimini, which evolved into *The Kiss*. Francesca had been married off against her will to Paolo's elder brother, the deformed Gianciotto, and he slew the couple in a jealous rage, after discovering them in a furtive embrace.

The subject had been depicted many times before — Dyce's version is a typical example (*see* Frontispiece). However, by stripping away all extraneous details, Rodin transformed the subject into a masterpiece, turning a trite literary anecdote into a timeless image of love.

PLATE 20

Pierre-Auguste Renoir
(1841–1919)
Dance in the Country

Renoir's abiding interest in observing the ways that Parisians enjoyed themselves led him to produce several pictures of dancing couples. This particular scene was one of a pair, in which he contrasted a country dance with its urban equivalent. However, this distinction was not all-important, as the artist also exhibited the paintings as *Summer* and *Winter*. Moreover, the 'country' location was scarcely rustic – it was actually Bougival, a popular riverside resort on the fringes of Paris.

Renoir used his friend Paul Lhote as the model for both male dancers, but he selected two different women to represent the partner. His 'city' dancer was the svelte and elegant Suzanne Valadon, a fellow-artist, while here he portrayed his new wife, Aline Charigot. Some critics commented unkindly on her ample figure, but the artist's devotion towards the young girl who brought such tenderness and harmony into his life is plain to see, making this a true painting of love.

PLATE 21

Walter Crane (1845—1915)
La Belle Dame sans Merci

DETAIL

The Victorians loved illustrating scenes from literature and the poetry of Keats provided them with one of their most fertile sources of inspiration. *La Belle Dame sans Merci*, with its subtle blend of medieval romance and implied menace, was a particular favourite. Here, Crane records with literal precision the trance-like rapture of the "pale knight", as he is lured into the forest by the mysterious lady with the flowing hair and wild eyes. This scene tallies closely with the following quatrain:

I set her on my pacing steed,
And nothing else saw all day long,
For sideways she would lean, and sing
A faery's song.

This idyllic mood will soon be shattered. The crescent moon shows that the day is drawing to an end and the knight is walking blindly to the "cold hill", where his fate will be sealed.

PLATE 22

Evelyn de Morgan (1855–1919)
Boreas and Orithyia

In Greek legend, Boreas was the personification of the North Wind and had long been in love with Orithyia. After repeated refusals, however, the angry suitor decided to take matters into his own hands and carried the damsel off to ravish her. Orithyia was associated with the goddess of Creation, and the myth relates to the ancient belief that children were the reincarnation of their ancestors and that conception was brought about by sudden gusts of wind.

Evelyn was fond of tackling obscure allegories of this kind — she produced another picture entitled *Boreas and the Fallen Leaves*, in which the latter were depicted as naked maidens. Her image of the Wind appears to have come directly from Ovid. He described the former's huge wings, which fanned the flames of his passion, and mentioned the long, dusty cloak which trailed behind him. The artist's personal style derived partly from the languid forms of Burne-Jones and partly from her obvious enthusiasm for the Florentine painters of the Renaissance.

PLATE 23
Gustav Klimt (1862−1918)
The Kiss

This intense, hypnotic picture is a potent image of full-blooded passion. Two lovers embrace on a flower-strewn patch of lawn. The woman is kneeling and her bare feet dangle precariously at the edge of a golden void. Despite this, the figures cling together so tightly that their bodies have merged into a single outline.

'The Kiss' was a popular subject among Symbolist artists at the turn of the century, but Klimt's version is highly individualistic. The rectangles and circles on the lovers' clothes have sexual overtones, and it should be remembered that Freud was both a direct contemporary and a fellow-citizen of Vienna. The theme of fertility is reinforced by the over-abundance of flowers and by the way that the man's ivy coronal is echoed in the golden strands of ivy that trail down from the woman's form. At the same time, there is something oppressive about the picture. The lovers seem cramped in their gilded space; the woman's head is tilted at a painful angle, and there is a vampiric quality about the couple's embrace.

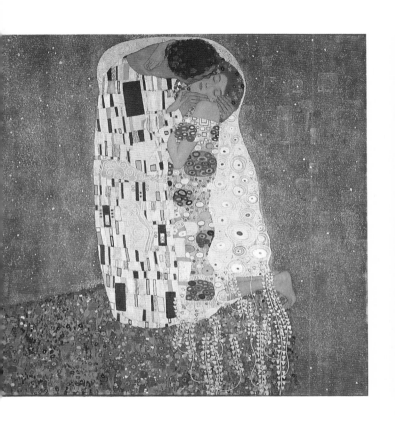

PLATE 24

Hugh Goldwin Riviere (1869–1956)
The Garden of Eden

This picture has no fanciful pretensions and aspires to do nothing more than portray an amorous young couple walking hand in hand. Here, the only concession to high art lies in the title. The reference to Eden is suggestive both of innocence and of the idea of a heaven on earth. The latter might seem ironic in view of the dismal weather, but the woman's rapt expression makes it plain that the paradise is in the lovers' minds. Even in the drizzle, this London scene can seem idyllic and the mood is enhanced by the misty evocation of such background details as a gas lamp, a pillar-box and a hansom cab.

The couple were Percy Silley and his fiancée, Beatrice Langdon-Davies, and the setting is Kensington Gardens. The composition is unusually elaborate for Riviere, doubtless because Beatrice was his sister-in-law. As they were unmarried at the time, the young lovers had to be rigorously chaperoned during the lengthy sittings.

PLATE 25

Marc Chagall (1887–1985)
The Bride and Groom

In the course of his long career, Chagall painted dozens of scenes of lovers or bridal couples, imbuing them with a spirit of poetic fancy. Sometimes, in their exuberance, the figures float in the sky and sometimes, as here, they glide along, weightless and dreamlike. Invariably, they are pictured in strange, chimerical settings, which transform the wedding into a magical event.

Chagall denied that he was a painter of fantasy, emphasizing that most of his images were drawn from childhood memories. Here, for example, the bandsmen are dressed in the garb of circus performers, whose antics had mesmerized him as a boy. The man with the bird's head plays a harp; the figure in the sky is a clarinettist; while, in the centre, stands the fiddler, the artist's favourite motif. The rooster signifies the dawn, which accounts for the purplish, early morning tones in the picture. By extension, this also alludes to the 'dawn' of the married life of the young couple.

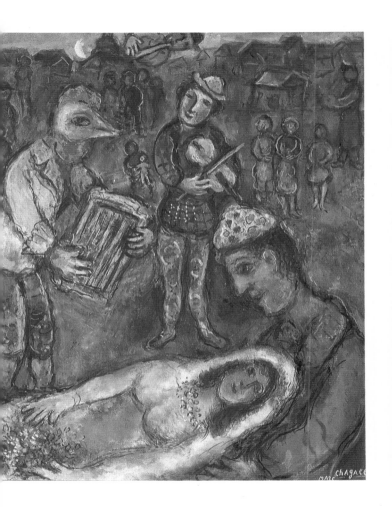

PICTURE ACKNOWLEDGEMENTS

The author and publishers would like to thank the following artists, collectors, galleries and photographic libraries for permission to reproduce their illustrations:

INTRODUCTION
Frontispiece: The National Gallery of Scotland, Edinburgh (Bridgeman Art Library, London)
The British Library, London
Kingston Lacy, Dorset (National Trust Photographic Library, London)
The British Library, London (Bridgeman Art Library)

PLATES
 1   S. Gimignano, Pinacoteca, Civica (Scala, Florence)
 2   Musée Cluny, Paris (Lauros-Giraudon/Bridgeman Art Library)
 3   The National Gallery, London
 4   The Metropolitan Museum of Art, New York (Bridgeman Art Library)
 5   Kunsthistorisches Museum, Vienna (Bridgeman Art Library)
 6   Courtesy of the Board of Trustees of the Victoria & Albert Museum, London
     (Bridgeman Art Library)
 7   Rijksmuseum, Amsterdam
 8   The National Gallery, London
 9   The Fitzwilliam Museum, Cambridge
10   Christie's, London (Bridgeman Art Library)
11   The Frick Collection, New York (Bridgeman Art Library)
12   Courtesy of the Board of Trustees of the Victoria & Albert Museum, London
     (Bridgeman Art Library)
13   Musée du Louvre, Paris (E. T. Archive, London)
14   The Whitworth Art Gallery, Manchester
15   Whitford & Hughes, London (Bridgeman Art Library)
16   & Cover (detail) Christie's, London (Bridgeman Art Library)
17   Birmingham City Museums & Art Gallery (Bridgeman Art Library)
18   Wightwick Manor, West Midlands (National Trust Photographic Library)
19   Private Collection (Bridgeman Art Library)
20   Musée d'Orsay, Paris (Giraudon/Bridgeman Art Library)
21   Christopher Wood Gallery, London (Bridgeman Art Library)
22   Cragside, Northumberland (National Trust Photographic Library)
23   Osterreichisches Galerie, Vienna (Bridgeman Art Library)
24   Guildhall Art Gallery, London (Bridgeman Art Library) © The Artist
25   Christie's, London (Bridgeman Art Library) © ADAGP, Paris and DACS, London 1994